Time for TEA

Ron Berger

Time for TEA

Ron Berger

Time for TEA

Time for TEA

No sweetner added

Ron Berger

**The Life saving effects of drinking TEA
are gained
drinking it straight**

Ron Berger

Time for TEA

Published by:

berger publishing

Rancho Belago, CA 92555
Email - mail@ronberger.com
Web Page - www.ronberger.com

berger publishing

Printed in the USA
ISBN 13 - 978-0-9799257-1-9
ISBN 10 - 0-9799257-1-1

First printing
Library of Congress Control Number: 2010921741

Ron Berger

Time for TEA

Ron's other books -

The House That Ron Built
(1-4137-8605-7) (978-1-4137-8605-7)
PublishAmerica, LLC

Are You Being Served Yet?
(1-4241-2485-9) (978-14241-2485-5)
PublishAmerica, LLC

P-NUT, The Love of a Dog
(1-59824-303-9) (978-1-59824-303-1)
E-Book Time, LLC

"Normal" MAYDAY
(0-9799257-0-3) (978-0-9799257-0-2)
berger publishing

Ron Berger

Time for TEA

Author's Note:

E-mail messages and article clips used in this
book are italicized and/or in bold with credit
given if the author and/or source is known.

I beseech everyone, who reads this book, to get
involved and to lend their voice in turning this
country around. I am not a member of the
"radical right" or the "right wing conspiracy" but
after reading this you will find that the "radical
left" and the "left wing conspiracy" is growing
fast.

Please also read the books by Sarah Palin and
Glenn Beck.

Join the TEA PARTY while it is still possible.

Ron Berger

Contents

About the author   8

Introduction   12

Basis for this book   17

All about Tea   21

Why now?   51

Replace the GOP?   57

Who should go?   61

How do we do it?   71

This Just In   103

ABOUT THE AUTHOR

Coming from a small town in Wisconsin, I was never exposed to much in the political realm. My dad was a Democrat, mainly because he was a union worker for the Electric Company, and he only looked for his benefits. My mother was a Republican (I think). Only one election did I get involved enough to actually offer my voting advise. It was 1948 when I heard Harry Truman talk and it made much more sense to me than Thomas Dewey that I advised my mother to vote for Truman. I don't know if she ever did, but Mr Truman was the last Democrat that made sense to me.

The election of 1952 was a no-brainer as far as I was concerned. I really felt sorry for Adlai Stevenson - and then for him to campaign against General

Eisenhower twice in four years was too much. Even the Democratic party tried to get Ike to run on their ticket in 1951. He was my Commander-in-Chief while I was in the USAF and I was proud of that fact.

My political life started to take shape when I was hired by a builder in California. That family was 100% Republican and you had better be also if you wanted to work for them. I didn't have to make any adjustment in my thinking and was on board with them from the first day. Nixon was our man and Kennedy was not. The next election in 1964 was Goldwater and not Johnson. We all know how those elections turned out.

During most Local, State and Federal elections I would automatically vote Republican. That doesn't mean that I thought they were better, but rather it was just easier. During the election of 1992 I broke that pattern and voted for Ross Perot. After he fell flat on his butt, I stopped voting altogether. I really couldn't tell the good from the bad. Oh, I had feelings, but figured that my vote didn't count anyway so why go through the hassle?

The last election between Obama and McCain really got me worked up. Not only did I feel this country now was going down the wrong path, but I felt an urgency about doing something about it. That's what most people felt, but didn't know what they should do about it. After about a year of receiving Obama bashing emails I realized that there has to be some truth to it. Then came the "Tea Party Brigades". I have never seen the general public so worked up and so wanting to turn this country around and take the control back from the Obama administration.

Now that a year has gone by with B. O. (Barack Obama) in charge, the meaning of "change" has really sunk in. He claimed that the USA was the best country in the world and he wanted to "change" it from the last administration. We now know that his change means socialism.

Lord, save us from those that think they know more than our founding fathers on how to run this country. This is the time for a complete change in Washington, DC. This is TEA TIME!

INTRODUCTION

I have read several books recently and have started several others. One book by Lee Iacocca *"Where Have all the Leaders Gone?"* is a shotgun approach to the Bush administration for all the stupid things that happened in eight years. I'm sure if he had waited several years to write his book, he would be focussing on the B.O. administration with much more meat to chew on. Bush had his shortcomings, but I truly believe he made a better president than Gore could have.

The next book is, *"Arguing with Idiots"* by Glenn Beck. One thing this book points out is that there are a great number of idiots in government. Glenn is not afraid to call a spade a spade and is not afraid to dig into many programs that the government has failed at completely and still pours money in to keep them afloat. This is a must reading for every conservative to understand just how incapable the federal government is at managing programs that they have no business getting into in the first place. If you don't feel sick to your stomach, then you didn't pay attention.

One of the best written and easily read books is *"Going Rogue"* by Sarah Palin. She is without a doubt, in my estimation, throughly qualified to run for president. Not only does she have much more experience than the present president, she can prove she is a "natural born citizen". That is something the present one hasn't done - as of this writing. And - if he can't prove it he deserves to be run out of Washington for lying to the American public and the World.

Sarah has shown that her ideas and beliefs are in line with the majority of citizens. She believes that the Tea Parties are a true representation of all God fearing and Country loving Americans. The Tea Party worked in 1773 and it's working in 2009/ 10.

Do not underestimate the power of Sarah Palin. She has sparked a fire that will turn into a blaze before 2012. Her 2008 Vice Presidential run was not a mistake as many in the Republican party claim. If she would have had more say in the campaign she might be in Washington today. Here are some interesting figures:

Professor Joseph Olson of Hamline University School of Law, St. Paul , Minnesota , points out some interesting facts concerning the 2008 Presidential election:

- Number of States won by: <u>Obama: 19</u>   <u>McCain: 29</u>
- Square miles of land won by: <u>Obama: 580,000</u>   <u>McCain: 2,427,000</u>

Population of counties won by: <u>Obama: 127 million</u>

<u>McCain: 143 million</u>
Murder rate per 100,000 residents in counties won by:
<u>Obama: 13.2</u>   <u>McCain: 2.1</u>

Professor Olson adds: "In aggregate, the map of the territory McCain won was mostly the land owned by the taxpaying citizens of the country.

Obama territory mostly encompassed those citizens living in low income tenements and living off various forms of government welfare..."

Olson believes the United States is now somewhere between the "complacency and apathy" phase of Professor Tyler's definition of democracy, with some forty percent of the nation's population already having reached the "governmental dependency" phase.

John McCain and Sarah Palin didn't lose - America lost. I believe we are now reaping what has been sown.

BASIS FOR THIS BOOK

When you read this book, there will be numerous emails and articles interjected to prove a point. Not all will agree with me, but there are a great number that will.

While planning this book, the two "Tea Parties" took my fancy and I became a member of both. I read about their March on Washington in 2009 and saw the pictures on TV and was intrigued why the B.O. Administration underplayed it as they did. Basically stating that the crowd size was far less than reality indicated. What were these people doing that shook up the boys in government? Maybe they were afraid that this idea might catch on and cause them problems.

Teapartypatriots.com and teapartynation.com are the two web addresses that deserve your attention. Before starting to write this book I formed a "group" designed primarily for our local community and the second day I had a member join that lives 3,000 miles away. This lady was promoting the Conservative candidate from Massachusetts, Scott Brown over Democrat Martha Coakley. Several days later Scott won and the Democrats started to blame Martha for not being a very good candidate. Not that what she stood for was wrong, but her personally. That's how the Republicans treated Sarah after the 2008 campaign.

You can now see that the main objective now is not being a Republican or Democrat, but rather whether you are a liberal or conservative. This is where the "Tea Parties" come in. They represent the conservative agenda and since the Republican party has been closely allied with conservatism in the past they are staying an arm of the party and not a separate entity.

The last true conservative Republican was Ronald Reagan. He turned this country around so we all could feel proud to be an American. He also played the biggest part in overcoming Communism. Truly a world leader. I believe God has brought Sarah to the forefront to be another Ronald Reagan. It's also about time for a woman to run the country. They are the only known species that can walk and chew gum at the same time.

ALL ABOUT TEA

The Boston Tea Party, 1773

Victory in the French and Indian War was costly for the British. At the war's conclusion in 1763, King George III and his government looked to taxing the American colonies as a way of recouping their war costs. They were also looking for ways to reestablish control over the colonial governments that had become increasingly independent while the Crown was distracted by the war. Royal ineptitude compounded the problem. A series of actions including the Stamp Act (1765), the Townsend Acts (1767) and the Boston Massacre (1770) agitated the colonists, straining relations with the mother country. But it was the Crown's attempt to tax tea that spurred the colonists to action and laid the groundwork

for the American Revolution.
<u>EyeWitnesstoHistory.com</u>

This is how it started. The British pushed the colonists to the breaking point and then they went into action. Tea is not something to go to war over, but the circumstances leading up to the tea were just to much.

It's been a year now since B.O. took over and the people are really getting tired of the excessive spending and the government taking over all aspects of our lives. We now have a debt that can't be repaid in our lifetimes. Our children and their children are now saddled with these bills. How can we teach our children to be thrifty and to spend their money wisely when the federal government keeps borrowing and printing money like it's going out of style. If they keep this up it will go out of style and a dollar wont be worth a plug nickel.

And another thing . . . The modern politically correct movement began at the University of Wisconsin-Madison; one of the most liberal institutions in the United States and is often viewed as a liberalist degrading of the freedom of speech. Being politically correct is really wearing on my nerves. That doesn't mean that you can call someone any name you wish, but you don't have to search the English language to find a word that won't offend them. If their skin is that thin, they need some toughening skills. Here is an example of the looniest derivative of a well known piece:

Christmas

A Politically Correct Christmas Poem

Twas the night before Christmas and Santa's a wreck...
How to live in a world that's politically correct?
His workers no longer would answer to "Elves",
"Vertically Challenged" they were calling themselves.
And labor conditions at the North Pole,
were alleged by the union, to stifle the soul.

Four reindeer had vanished without much propriety,
released to the wilds, by the Humane Society.
And equal employment had made it quite clear,

that Santa had better not use just reindeer.
So Dancer and Donner, Comet and Cupid,
were replaced with 4 pigs, and you know
that looked stupid!

The runners had been removed from his
beautiful sleigh,
because the ruts were deemed dangerous
by the EPA,
And millions of people were calling the
Cops,
when they heard sled noises upon their
roof tops.
Second-hand smoke from his pipe, had
his workers quite frightened,
and his fur trimmed red suit was called
"unenlightened".

To show you the strangeness of today's
ebbs and flows,
Rudolf was suing over unauthorized use
of his nose.
He went to Geraldo, in front of the Nation,
demanding millions in over-due workers
compensation.

So...half of the reindeer were gone, and
his wife
who suddenly said she'd had enough of

this life,
joined a self help group, packed and left in a whiz,
demanding from now on that her title was Ms.

And as for gifts...why, he'd never had the notion
that making a choice could cause such commotion.
Nothing of leather, nothing of fur...
Which meant nothing for him or nothing for her.
Nothing to aim, Nothing to shoot,
Nothing that clamored or made lots of noise.
Nothing for just girls and nothing for just boys.
Nothing that claimed to be gender spe-cific,
Nothing that's warlike or non-pacifistic.

No candy or sweets...they were bad for the tooth.
Nothing that seemed to embellish upon the truth.
And fairy tales...while not yet forbidden,
were like Ken and Barbie, better off hid-den,
for they raised the hackles of those psy-chological,

who claimed the only good gift was one ecological.

No baseball, no football...someone might get hurt,
besides - playing sports exposed kids to dirt.
Dolls were said to be sexist and should be passe.
and Nintendo would rot your entire brain away.

So Santa just stood there, disheveled and perplexed,
he just couldn't figure out what to do next?
He tried to be merry he tried to be gay,
but you must have to admit he was having a very bad day.
His sack was quite empty, it was flat on the ground,
nothing fully acceptable was anywhere to be found.

Something special was needed, a gift that he might,
give to us all, without angering the left or the right.
A gift that would satisfy - with no indecision,
each group of people in every religion.

Every race, every hue,
everyone, everywhere...even you!
So here is that gift, it's price beyond
worth...

"MAY YOU AND YOUR LOVED ONES,
ENJOY PEACE ON EARTH"

One more for good measure . . .

A Politically Correct Christmas Greeting

Best wishes for an environmentally conscious, socially responsible, low stress, non-addictive, gender neutral, winter solstice holiday, practiced within the most joyous traditions of the religious persuasion of your choice, but with respect for the religious persuasion of others who choose to practice their own religion as well as those who choose not to practice a religion at all.

Something we should all memorize, don't you think?

<u>And another thing</u> . . .I get nauseated when I hear Black people call themselves "African Americans". Most of us originated from other countries, of course a number of generations removed, so why do they still want to be known as African Americans when most people call themselves just "Americans". Most African Americans don't know where Africa is and surely haven't been there. If they were born in America, then they are Americans - period. There is nothing wrong with the name, Black - especially when they call us Caucasians, White. Wake up people. Quit thinking that you're special and feeling sorry for yourselves. You just need to live up to your "American heritage".

An example of political correctness is the changing terminology used to described handicapped people. In the past the term "crippled" was perfectly acceptable and not considered offensive. At some point, Americans like Senate Republican Leader Bob Dole decided "crippled" was degrading and the preferred term changed to "handicapped". This, too, was eventually deemed offensive and "disabled" became the preferred term. Today, "disabled" is now considered degrading and "differently abled" and "physically challenged" are now the politically correct terms.

The same can be said for the changing uses of terms for Black Americans: "Negro" and "colored", once perfectly acceptable terms, became offensive during the 1970s and "Afro-American" and "Black" came into use, which in turn gave way to "African-American", and in broader usage, "people of color".

The more "correct" you are, the stupider it sounds.

<u>And another thing</u> . . . Congress should not vote for something that they do not participate in. This is leading to a very large, angry group demanding that the following be implemented as soon as possible:

For too long we have been too complacent about the workings of Congress. Many citizens had no idea that Congress members could retire with the same pay after only one term, that they didn't pay into Social Security, that they specifically exempted them-selves from many of the laws they have passed (such as being exempt from any fear of prosecution for sexual harassment) while ordinary citizens must live under those laws. The latest is to exempt themselves from the Healthcare Reform that is being considered...in all of its' forms. Somehow, that doesn't seem logical. We do not have an elite that is above the law. I truly don't care if they are Democrat, Republican, Independent or whatever. The self-serving must stop. This is a good way to do that. It is an idea whose time has come.

Proposed 28th Amendment to the United States Constitution:

"Congress shall make no law that applies to the citizens of the United States that does not apply equally to the Senators and Representatives; and, Congress shall make no law that applies to the Senators and Representatives that does not apply equally to the citizens of the United States ".

Don't you think this is right?

Actually I believe the following is a great representation of how effective the government is in managing agencies that they have decreed to exist. Here is an example:

CONGRESS BEWARE!

WE, THE PEOPLE, ARE WATCHING.

WE'LL SEE YOU AT THE NEXT ELECTION.

For those of you in Congress who need us to paint pictures:

The U.S. Postal Service was established in 1775 - you have had 234 years to get it right; it is now broke.
Social Security was established in 1935 - you have had 74 years to get it right; it is now broke.

Fannie Mae was established in 1938 - you have had 71 years to get it right; it is now broke.

The "War on Poverty" started in 1964 - you have had 45 years to get it right; $1 trillion of our money is confiscated each year and transferred to "the poor"; it hasn't worked and our entire country is now broke.

Medicare and Medicaid were established in 1965 - you've had 44 years to get it right; they are now broke.

Freddie Mac was established in 1970 - you have had 39 years to get it right; it is now broke.

Trillions of dollars were spent in the massive political payoffs called TARP, the "Stimulus," the Omnibus Appropriations Act of 2009...none of which show any signs of working, although ACORN appears to have found a new source: the American taxpayer.

And finally, to set a new record:

"Cash for Clunkers" was established in 2009 and went broke in 2009! It took older cars (that were the best some people could afford) and replaced them with higher-priced and less-affordable cars, mostly Japanese. A good percentage of the profits went out of the country and the American taxpayers take the hit for Congress' generosity in burning three billion more of our dollars on failed experiments.

So with a perfect 100% failure rate and a record that proves that the "services" you shove down our throats are failing faster and faster, and you want Americans to believe you can be *trusted with a government-run health care system?*

20% of our entire economy?

With all due respect do you think we are crazy?

Or better still

Are you crazy?

And - just a little more to add insult to injury:

Another reminder to join the November 2010 movement to vote them all out.
  GRRRRRRRRR....!
I'm MAD AND YOU WILL BE TOO!

  Your U.S. House & Senate have voted themselves $4,700 and $5,300 raises.
1.   *They voted to not give you a S.S. cost of living raise in 2010 and 2011.*

2.	Your	Medicaid	premiums
will	go	up $285.60 for	the	2-
years and you will not get the 3%
COLA:
$660/yr. Your total 2-yr loss and
cost	is	-$1,600	or	-$3,200 for
husband and wife

3.	Over	2-yrs The	House	&
Senate each get $10,000 raises

4.	Do you feel SCREWED?

5.	WILL your	cost	of	drugs	-
doctor fees - local taxes - food,
etc.,	increase?	You	better	be-
lieve they will!

WILL	THEIRS...NO	WAY . They	have
a	raise and better benefits. Why
care	about	you? You	never	did
anything about it in the past.
You're	obviously	too	stupid
or don't	care. No	offense; just
making a point!

6.   *Do you really think that Nancy, Harry, Chris, Charlie, Barnie, et al, care about you?*

SEND THE MESSAGE-- You're FIRED.

Now there's a message I can believe in.

<u>And another thing</u> . . .The ACLU (American Civil Liberties Union) really is annoying. They have to be the ONE power in the United States that is responsible for the reduction of God's presence. This country was founded on God being the center of the universe and the staple for our country. How dare these "lawyers" demand that God step aside. They are very representative of the present B.O. Administration and congress. Nancy Pelosi was rumored to have said that " . . *You don't need God anymore, you have us Democrats"*. Doesn't that just make you sick? Many things have

been said about Nancy. One statement came from Jack Cafferty from CNN. Here is the web address where you can see and hear this video: http://www.realclearpolitics.com/video/2010/01/12/jack_cafferty_on_nancy_pelosi_what_a_horrible_woman.html

His statement at the end says it all. "Nancy Pelosi, what a horrible woman". I don't think it can get any plainer than that. Plus - Jack is from CNN. One of the news stations that are "in the pocket" of the Democratic party. Maybe the press is beginning to see the light and will start to tell it the way it really is and without rose colored glasses.

<u>And another (last)thing</u> . . .

The Problem Is Identified.........LAWYERS

Johnny Carson nailed lawyers with one of his "how cold was it?" jokes! "It was so cold that lawyers were running around with their hands in their own pockets!!"

This is very interesting! I never thought about it this way.
Perhaps this is why so many physicians are conservatives or republicans.

The Democratic Party has become the Lawyers' Party.
Barack Obama is a lawyer.
Michelle Obama is a lawyer.
Hillary Clinton is a lawyer.
Bill Clinton is a lawyer.
John Edwards is a lawyer.
Elizabeth Edwards is a lawyer.

Every Democrat nominee since 1984 went to law school (although Gore did not graduate).

Every Democrat vice presidential nominee since 1976, except for Lloyd Bentsen, went to law school.

Look at leaders of the Democrat Party in Congress:

Harry Reid is a lawyer.
Nancy Pelosi is a lawyer.

The Republican Party is different.
President Bush is a businessman.
Vice President Cheney is a businessman.
The leaders of the Republican Revolution:
Newt Gingrich was a history professor.
Tom Delay was an exterminator.
Dick Armey was an economist.
House Minority Leader Boehner was a plastic manufacturer.
The former Senate Majority Leader Bill Frist is a heart surgeon.

Who was the last Republican president who was a lawyer? Gerald Ford, who left office 31 years ago and who barely won the Republican nomination as a sitting president, running against Ronald Reagan in 1976. The Republican Party is made up of real people doing real work, who are often the targets of lawyers.

The Democrat Party is made up of lawyers. Democrats mock and scorn men who create wealth, like Bush and Cheney, or who heal the sick, like Frist, or who immerse themselves in history, like Gingrich.

The Lawyers' Party sees these sorts of people, who provide goods and services that people want, as the enemies of America . And, so we have seen the procession of official enemies, in the eyes of the Lawyers' Party, grow.

Against whom do Hillary and Obama rail? Pharmaceutical companies, oil companies, hospitals, manufacturers, fast food restaurant chains, large retail businesses, bankers, and anyone producing anything of value in our nation.

This is the natural consequence of viewing everything through the eyes of lawyers. Lawyers solve problems by successfully representing their clients, in this case the American people. Lawyers seek to have new laws passed, they seek to win lawsuits, they press appellate courts to overturn precedent, and lawyers always parse language to favor their side.

Confined to the narrow practice of law, that is fine. But it is an awful way to govern a great nation. When politicians as lawyers begin to view some Americans as clients and other Americans as opposing parties, then the role of the legal system in our life becomes all-consuming. Some Americans become "adverse parties" of our very government. We are not all litigants in some vast social class-action suit. We are citizens of a republic that promises us a great deal of freedom from laws, from courts, and from lawyers.

Today, we are drowning in laws; we are contorted by judicial decisions; we are driven to distraction by omnipresent lawyers in all parts of our once private lives. America has a place for laws and lawyers, but that place is modest and reasonable, not vast and unchecked. When the most important decision for our next president is whom he will appoint to the Supreme Court, the role of lawyers and the law in America is too big. When lawyers use criminal prosecution as a continuation of politics by other means, as happened in the lynching of Scooter Libby and Tom Delay, then the power of lawyers in America is too great. When House Democrats sue America in order to hamstring our efforts to learn what our enemies are planning to do to us, then the role of litigation in America has become crushing.

We cannot expect the Lawyers' Party to provide real change, real reform or real hope in America. Most Americans know that a republic in which every major government action must be blessed by nine unelected judges is not what Washington intended in 1789. Most Americans grasp that we cannot fight a war when ACLU lawsuits snap at the heels of our defenders. Most Americans intuit that more lawyers and judges will not restore declining moral val-

ues or spark the spirit of enterprise in our economy.

Perhaps Americans will understand that change cannot be brought to our nation by those lawyers who already largely dictate American society and business. Perhaps Americans will see that hope does not come from the mouths of lawyers but from personal dreams nourished by hard work. Perhaps Americans will embrace the truth that more lawyers with more power will only make our problems worse.

The United States has 5% of the world's population and 66% of the world's lawyers! Tort (Legal) reform legislation has been introduced in congress several times in the last several years to limit punitive damages in ridiculous lawsuits such as "spilling hot coffee on yourself and suing the establishment that sold it to you" and also to limit punitive damages in huge medical malpractice lawsuits. This legislation has continually been blocked from even being voted on by the Democrat Party. When you see that 97% of the political contributions from the American Trial Lawyers Association goes to the Democrat Party, then you realize who is responsible for our medical and product costs being so high!

Maybe that's the key to our problems. Check out the ballot next time you vote and if you see "Lawyer" listed as an occupation to a potential candidate - pass him/her over. We don't need any more lawyers in Washington.

These are just a few of the things that have led me up to the point of this book. We Americans are gluttons for punishment, but when the cup of tolerance is full we seem to bust out and change things. The government hasn't figured that out yet and have let the cup overflow. Now they have to bear the brunt of the storm. Even the "good" people in Congress are subject to the Tea Party actions. Kind of like The Lord sends rain on the good and the bad. All will feel the cleansing vote of the people.

The Crotch Salute Returns

I'm sure you remember this one.

I'm sorry folks, but is this the turkey that was elected President of our country? You know, the United States of America ? I do believe that saluting the flag goes with that, and also to honor the servicemen who died, or is he above that? Shower us all with flowery words and dazzle us with B.S. but actions speak louder.

This President continues to insult OUR country and OUR military.

PROUD MEMBER OF THE

Angry Mob

If you're not outraged, you're not paying attention.

FOR REAL CHANGE VOTE OUT YOUR CONGRESSMAN IN 2010 !!!

2010

I WANT YOU

to throw the bums out!

Amendment 28

Congress shall NOT be exempt
from legislation imposed
on the rest of America

Why Now?

Why not now? If we don't act fast, we may be to late. This "TEA Movement" needs to take hold and start running. The 2010 elections are less than a year away and the "contestants" need to know if they have a chance or not. We need to continue the Massachusetts Senate race outcome in many more places.

This isn't a battle between Republican and Democrat, but rather between Conservative and Liberal. We have some conservative Democrats as well as liberal Republicans. We really need to know how they stand on this issue before we cast our vote. The only way we will turn our country around is to have as many conservatives in office as possible. The liberals have already given the farm away and we need to get it back. We need to get back to common sense and level headed thinking. Throwing money at all our problems is not the answer. In most all cases the problem only got worse so not only did we have a failed program, but lost all the money as well. Here is a email that says it all:

2010 is an election year for 1/3 of the senate and all of the house of representatives. It would be nice if congress got the message; the voting taxpayers are in charge now.

Social Security 2010

LET US SHOW OUR LEADERS IN WASHINGTON "PEOPLE POWER" AND THE POWER OF THE INTERNET.

IT DOESN'T MATTER IF YOU ARE RE-PUBLICAN OR DEMOCRAT!

START A BILL TO PLACE ALL POLI-TICIANS ON SOCIAL SECURITY

Perhaps we are asking the wrong questions during election years.

Our Senators and Congresswomen do not pay into Social Security and, of course,they do not collect from it.

You see, Social Security benefits were not suitable for persons of their rare elevation in society. They felt they should have a special plan for themselves So, many years ago they voted in their own benefit plan.

In more recent years,no congress person has felt the need to change it.
After all, it is a great plan.

For all practical purposes their plan works like this:

When they retire, they continue to draw the same pay until they die..!

Except it may increase from time to time for cost of living adjustments...

For example, Senator Byrd and Congressman White and their wives may expect to draw $7, 800,000.00 (that's Seven Million, Eight-Hundred Thousand Dollars), with their wives drawing $275, 000.00 during the last years of their lives. This is calculated on an average life span for each of those two Dignitaries.

Younger Dignitaries
who retire at an early age,
will receive much more during the rest of their lives.

Their cost for this excellent plan is $0.00... ZIP!! NADA!!! ZILCH!!!

This little perk they voted for themselves is FREE to them.

You and I pick up the tab for this plan. The funds for this fine retirement plan come directly from the General Funds;

"OUR TAX DOLLARS AT WORK"!

From our own Social Security Plan, which you and I pay
(or have paid) into, every payday until we retire (which amount is matched by our employer),
We can expect to get an average of $1,000 per month after retirement. Or, in other words,
we would have to collect our average of $1,000 monthly benefits for 68 years and one (1) month to equal Senator Bill Bradley's benefits!

Social Security could be very good if only one small change were made. That change would be to Jerk the Golden Fleece Retirement Plan from under the Senators and Congressmen... Put

them into the Social Security plan with the rest of us,
Then sit back..... And see how fast they would fix it!

Replace the GOP?

NO. To act as a separate political party would be a disaster. Working within the Republican Party is the only way to go. You will already find more conservatives in the GOP than the Democrats. It has shown itself in prior years that splinter parties only dilute the vote. As a good example; 1992 and Ross Perot's party (I forgot what they called it). It was very possible if Ross wasn't involved, George H.W. Bush may have spent another four years in the white house. Then consider what would have happened with Clinton and George W. Bush. It is extremely possible that his royal highness, BO, would not be where he is today. I guess we can blame most of our problems on Ross Perot.

We have to get the main body GOP on the conservative band wagon and do our best to prove, to everyone, that it's the only way to go to get us on the right track again.

The Republicans of the past have been able to turn things around and make us feel proud to live in the USA again. Ike and Ronald Reagan were two of those that grabbed the problem by the balls and made it go away. Reagan was the trigger that made the Soviet Union go away after we had engaged in a cold war with them for over 40 years. The Iron Curtain was dismantled and people were united with their family and loved ones again. Countries became one and travel opened up and people could breath easier. I don't know if President Reagan knew how everything would turn out, but I know that he had faith in our system and in the people to accomplish this, seemingly, impossible mission. He saluted the flag and cared about his fellow citizens and knew that to make the world better, the USSR had to be defeated without a hot war. If you ever get to the Ronald Reagan Library in Simi Valley, CA, take a look at a section of the iron curtain. It will give you some feeling of what life was like behind this barricade.

Who should go?

Maybe it's time for........
Amendment 28

"Congress shall make no law that applies to the citizens of the United States that does not apply equally to the Senators or Representatives,and Congress shall make no law that applies to the Senators or Representatives that does not apply equally to the citizens of the United States ."

Let's get this passed around, - these people in Washington have brought this upon themselves!!! It's time for retribution. Let's take back America.

Here are some more emails that tell how loved some of our Congressional members really are:

Mathew Staver, Founder and Chairman Liberty Counsel

You and I have just witnessed one of the most corrupt legislative sessions in American history. Now we have learned that one of the key "experts" pushing ObamaCare was also bought and paid for!

The New York Times has exposed Jonathan Gruber, a professor of economics at M.I.T., as having published an article on their Op-Ed page supporting ObamaCare without disclosing that he had an ongoing consulting relationship with HHS.
The Times noted that Professor Gruber had signed a contract obligating him to reveal such relationships. It would have

been impossible for him to "forget" his consultancy - he had nearly $400,000 worth of lucrative contracts with HHS at the time!

++But wait - it gets much, much worse...

Popular blog site Firedoglake revealed last Friday that the Obama Administration has paid Gruber more than $780,000 in TAX DOLLARS to make the public case for health care reform!

Jonathan Gruber's work has been extensively cited by the White House, Members of Congress, and the media continuously since ObamaCare came onto the scene, but NOT ONCE did anyone in the administration disclose he was on their payroll!

Here's Gruber's lame explanation: "All my editorials or public reports have been done on my own time." I guess he expects us to believe that his views weren't influenced by the nearly one million dollars he's gotten so far!

++More "Chicago on the Potomac"

The Jonathan Gruber revelation is just the latest public exposure of the graft and dishonesty which has characterized the way the Obama/Pelosi/Reid power axis has advanced ObamaCare. Given what we know, can you imagine what else is under the table?!

Just before Christmas, Senate Majority Leader Harry Reid systematically bought off every Democrat member of the Senate who could possibly derail his crucial cloture vote. When all the "bribes" were handed out, Reid had the required 60 votes to choke off debate in the middle of the night.

The congressional leadership and the Obama White House arm twisters have literally drug our nation down to the level of a cheap banana republic! They know their popular support is *plummeting. They have become desperate and will stop at nothing.*

Honest Americans have been nauseated as we have learned:

** Senator Mary Landrieu (D-LA) received $300 million in extra
federal spending for her state in what critics derisively
called "The Louisiana Purchase."

** Senator Ben Nelson (D-NE) accepted a deal exempting his state
from new Medicaid costs and several other long-term perks.

Nelson's purchase has been dubbed the "Cornhusker Kick Back."

** Many other bribes and "special provisions" affected the states
of Vermont, North and South Dakota, Wyoming, Massachusetts,
Hawaii, Michigan, Florida, and Connecticut.

But perhaps most painful of all, we have watched a smug Harry Reid justifying his corrupt acts by suggesting it is every senator's DUTY to get pay-offs for their votes!

"If they don't have something in it important to them, then it doesn't speak well of them," Reid said in a post-cloture interview. So much for the integrity of the United States Senate!

++On top of all the corruption, ObamaCare is unconstitutional

If you wondered why Harry Reid rushed his 2,074-page bill and its 383-page "Manager's Amendment" through in the middle of the night with just hours to read them, then here's at least one answer...

Right there on page 1,020, the tyrannical Senate majority insists that no future Congress can repeal or otherwise amend the section on "Independent Medical Advisory Boards."

You will probably remember that socialists mocked Governor Sarah Palin for calling such independent boards "death panels." Yet

Governor Palin was correct in her assessment - what else would you call boards with the power to grant or deny life-saving care using some pseudo-scientific "cost-benefit" formula?

Carefully hidden away in Reid's version of ObamaCare is a section that gives these boards far more power and permanence than the Constitution allows to ANY government entity!

++ If this bill becomes law, Liberty Counsel will challenge its constitutionality in court!

Every version of ObamaCare we've seen so far is unconstitutional because:

1) Congress has NO authority to force every American to carry insurance coverage, and,

2) Congress has NO authority to fine employers whose policies do not have the mandated coverage.

If this monstrous healthcare bill passes, it must be strongly challenged in the federal judiciary from the moment of its birth. Liberty Counsel will do exactly that!

++But for now, especially since there is an increasing outcry against ObamaCare's corruption, we MUST continue to make Congress hear our voice!

We are going all out to BURY Congress in protest over this endless procession of dirty tricks. And it looks like ObamaCare is more vulnerable than ever due to the recent sordid revelations of bribery and scandal.

Americans nationwide are expressing OUTRAGE at this overt manipulation and total lack of integrity. Reid, Pelosi and Obama have proven they will do anything to get this government takeover of our medical industry. Now more than ever, the socialists and abortion advocates need to understand that *WE HAVE NOT GIVEN UP* and will resist to the very end! If Reid loses one vote in the Senate or Pelosi three or four in the House, then ObamaCare will not pass!

Pray for God's deliverance from being forced to pay for abortions and from the overt deceit and trickery that has become the norm from the Obama/Pelosi/Reid power axis. PLEASE keep the heat on, especially now that we have been shoved aside!

This battle is not over, no matter how much the Pelosi/Reid/Obama power axis wants us to think that it is. Now that there are nearly daily revelations of corruption and a number of serious challenges to ObamaCare's constitutionality, anything can happen!

Please pray! There is always hope in God! Continue taking action! And let your Senators know that you WILL hold them account-

able for their decisions on ObamaCare and its outrageous han-
dling!

How Do We Do It?

First and foremost, we PRAY! We pray that God will give us strength to carry on this fight and ultimately win the battle. We have to return God as the center of our universe and our country. We need to get prayer back in schools and bible verses back on walls and monuments where they were before the ACLU got so much power to have them removed.

This is not to promote religion but rather to put God back in charge or our destiny. A bible verse worth keeping: *"Blessed is the nation whose God is the Lord"*, Psalms, 33:12. We need God to heal our country and set it on the right path. Even if you are not strong in the religious part, you have to admit that our country was founded on God being the center. We have to get back to this feeling again to make things right. Another bible verse that we need to take to heart:

"If my people, which are called by my name, shall humble themselves and pray and seek my face and turn from their wicked ways; then will I hear from heaven and will forgive their sin and will heal their land." 2 Chronicles 7:14. These are not just empty sayings. God has always kept His promises and we have no reason to doubt Him now.

Our land certainly needs healing. Government is out of control, money is being spent with no accountability, regulations are being imposed without their consequences being studied, government is getting involved in companies and programs that they have proved before they are incapable of succeeding and our representatives are demonstrating that they know better than the people they are supposed to represent. Corruption and self centered thinking are creating a government that is far removed from the mandate that was set out in the constitution and bill of rights.

Second, we need to vote for the very best person. This should mean that the person should be conservative and not be so beholden to any party or group that want the wrong kind of change. The change that was voted on in 2008 was the wrong kind and it didn't take long to figure that out. We are now beholding to the Chinese and who knows what other country owns us.

Third, we need to really make the effort to get rid of the really bad Democrats that now seem to be "in power". This next email is an illustration:

Quote Of The Week
"Frankly, I don't know what it is about California, but we seem to

have a strange urge to elect really obnoxious women to high office. I'm not bragging, you understand, but no other state, including Maine, even comes close. When it comes to sending left-wing dingbats to Washington, we're number one. There's no getting around the fact that the last time anyone saw the likes of Barbara Boxer, Dianne Feinstein and Nancy Pelosi, they were stirring a cauldron when the curtain went up on 'Macbeth'. The three of them are like jackasses who happen to possess the gift of speech. You don't know if you should condemn them for their stupidity or simply marvel at their ability to form words."
--columnist Burt Prelutsky

That doesn't speak well for California. I'm sure that we could do a lot better. The only "experience" they really have is spending money.

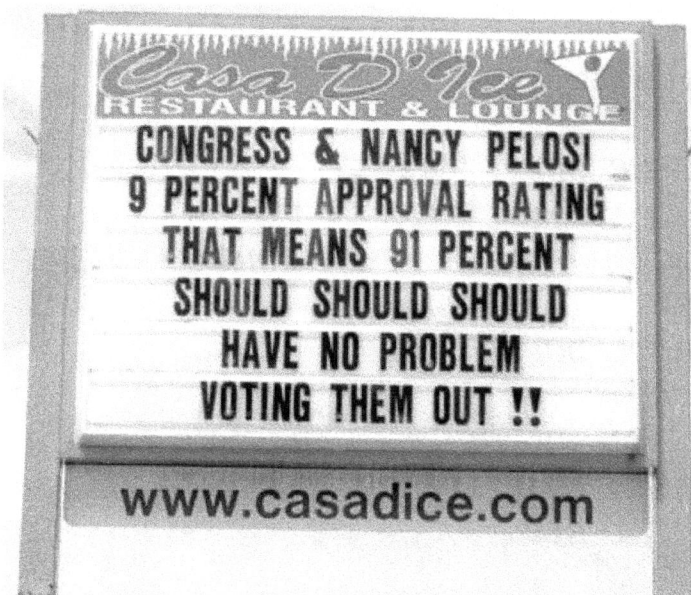

CONGRESS & NANCY PELOSI
9 PERCENT APPROVAL RATING
THAT MEANS 91 PERCENT
SHOULD SHOULD SHOULD
HAVE NO PROBLEM
VOTING THEM OUT !!

www.casadice.com

I must speak a little bit about illegal immigration. Our borders are like sieves and trying to keep illegals out has not been productive. Our problem is not so much that so many people want to come to the USA, but they want all the benefits associated with this illegal activity. No other country has the problem that we do and it all has to do with giving them so many incentives to cross the border.

LET ME SEE IF I GOT THIS RIGHT.

IF YOU CROSS THE NORTH KOREAN BORDER ILLEGALLY YOU GET 12 YEARS HARD LABOR.

IF YOU CROSS THE IRANIAN BORDER ILLEGALLY YOU ARE DETAINED INDEFINITELY.

IF YOU CROSS THE AFGHAN BORDER ILLEGALLY, YOU GET SHOT.

IF YOU CROSS THE SAUDI ARABIAN BORDER ILLEGALLY YOU WILL BE JAILED.

IF YOU CROSS THE CHINESE BORDER ILLEGALLY YOU MAY NEVER BE HEARD FROM AGAIN.

IF YOU CROSS THE VENEZUELAN BORDER ILLEGALLY YOU WILL BE BRANDED A SPY AND

YOUR FATE WILL BE SEALED..

*IF YOU CROSS THE CUBAN BORDER IL-
LEGALLY YOU WILL BE THROWN INTO
POLITICAL
PRISON TO ROT.*

*IF YOU CROSS THE U.S. BORDER IL-
LEGALLY YOU GET
* A JOB,
* A DRIVERS LICENSE,
* SOCIAL SECURITY CARD,
* WELFARE,
* FOOD STAMPS,
* CREDIT CARDS,
* SUBSIDIZED RENT OR A LOAN TO
BUY A HOUSE,
* FREE EDUCATION,
* FREE HEALTH CARE,
* A LOBBYIST IN WASHINGTON
* BILLIONS OF DOLLARS WORTH OF
PUBLIC DOCUMENTS PRINTED IN YOUR
   LANGUAGE
* THE RIGHT TO CARRY YOUR COUN-
TRY'S FLAG WHILE YOU PROTEST THAT
YOU DON'T GET ENOUGH RESPECT
* AND, IN MANY INSTANCES WITH A*

LITTLE HELP FROM "ACORN", YOU CAN VOTE.

I JUST WANTED TO MAKE SURE I HAD A FIRM GRASP ON THE SITUATION.

I don't recommend copying those other countries penalties for crossing their borders, but you can easily see that if we stop making it so comfortable to do so the traffic will slow down.

I must also put in a word to all who believe that Islam is a religion that "just wants peace". Here is the German point of view:

This is by far the best explanation of the Muslim terrorist situation I have ever read. The references to past history are accurate and clear. Not long, easy to understand, and well worth the read. The author of this email is Paul E. Marek.

A German's View on Islam

A man, whose family was German aristocracy prior to World War II, owned a number of large industries and estates. When asked how many German people were true Nazis, the answer he gave can guide our attitude toward fanaticism.

"Very few people were true Nazis,' he said, 'but many enjoyed the return of German pride, and many more were too busy to care. I was one of those who just thought the Nazis were a bunch of fools. So, the majority just sat back and let it all happen.

Then, before we knew it, they owned us, and we had lost control, and the end of the world had come.

My family lost everything. I ended up in a concentration camp and the Allies destroyed my factories".

We are told again and again by 'experts' and 'talking heads' that Islam is the religion of peace, and that the vast majority of Muslims just want to live in peace. Although this unqualified assertion may be true, it is entirely irrelevant.

It is meaningless fluff, meant to make us feel better, and meant to somehow diminish the spectra of fanatics rampaging across the globe in the name of Islam.

The fact is that the fanatics rule Islam at this moment in history. It is the fanatics who march. It is the fanatics who wage any one of 50 shooting wars worldwide. It is the fanatics who systematically slaughter Christian or tribal groups throughout Africa and are gradually taking over the entire continent in an Islamic wave. It is the fanatics who bomb, behead, murder or honor-kill. It is the fanatics who take over mosque after mosque. It is the fanatics who zealously spread the stoning and hanging of rape victims and homosexuals. It is the fanatics who teach their young to kill and to become suicide bombers.

The hard quantifiable fact is, that the peaceful majority, the 'silent majority' , is cowed and extraneous.

Communist Russia was comprised of Russians who just wanted to live in peace, yet the Russian Communists were responsible for the murder of about 20 million people. The peaceful majority were irrelevant.

China's huge population was peaceful as well, but Chinese

Communists managed to kill a staggering 70 million people.

The average Japanese individual prior to World War II was not a war mongering sadist Yet, Japan murdered and slaughtered its way across South East Asia in an orgy of killing that included the systematic murder of 12 million Chinese civilians; most killed by sword, shovel, and bayonet.

And who can forget Rwanda, which collapsed into butchery. Could it not be said that the majority of Rwandans were 'peace loving'?

History lessons are often incredibly simple and blunt, yet for all our powers of reason we often miss the most basic and uncomplicated of points: Peace-loving Muslims have been made irrelevant by their silence. Peace-loving Muslims will become our enemy if they don't speak up, because like my friend from Germany, they will awaken one day and find that the fanatics own them, and the end of their world will have begun.

Peace-loving Germans, Japanese, Chinese, Russians, Rwandans, Serbs, Afghans, Iraqis, Palestinians, Somalis, Nigerians, Algerians and many others have died because the peaceful majority did not speak up until it was too late.

As for us who watch it all unfold, we must pay attention to the only group that counts; the fanatics who threaten our way of life.

Lastly, anyone who doubts that the issue is serious and just deletes this email without sending it on is contributing to the passiveness that allows the problems to expand. So, extend yourself a *bit and send this on and on and on! Let us hope that thousands, world wide, read this and think about it, and send it on before it's too late.*

The first thing the fanatics will do to the silent majority is to disarm them.

Not even Australia wants them around if they don't like their ways.

This man should be appointed King of the World. Truer words have never been spoken.

It took a lot of courage for this man to speak what he had to say for the world to hear. The retribution could be phenomenal, but at least he was willing to take a stand on his and Australia's beliefs.
Whole world Needs A Leader Like This!

Muslims who want to live under Islamic Sharia law were told on Wednesday to get out of Australia , as the government targeted radicals in a bid to head off potential terror attacks..

Separately, Rudd angered some Australian Muslims on Wednesday by saying he supported spy agencies monitoring the nation's mosques. Quote:
'IMMIGRANTS, NOT AUSTRALIANS, MUST ADAPT. Take It Or Leave It. I am tired of this nation worrying about whether we are offending some individual or their culture. Since the terrorist attacks on Bali , we have experienced a surge in patriotism by the majority of Australians. '

'This culture has been developed over two centuries of struggles, trials and victories by millions of men and women who have sought freedom'

'We speak mainly ENGLISH, not Spanish, Lebanese, Arabic, Chinese, Japanese, Russian, or any other language. Therefore, if you wish to become part of our society . Learn the language!'

'Most Australians believe in God. This is not some Christian, right wing, political push, but a fact, because Christian men and women, on Christian principles, founded this nation, and this is clearly documented. It is certainly appropriate to display it on the walls of our schools. If God offends you, then I suggest you consider another part of the world as your new home, because God is part of our culture.'

'We will accept your beliefs, and will not question why. All we ask is that you accept ours, and live in harmony and peaceful enjoyment with us.'

'This is OUR COUNTRY, OUR LAND, and OUR LIFESTYLE, and we will allow you every opportunity to enjoy all this. But once you are done complaining, whining, and griping about Our Flag, Our Pledge, Our Christian beliefs, or Our Way of Life, I highly encourage you take advantage of one other great Australian freedom, 'THE RIGHT TO LEAVE'.'

'If you aren't happy here then LEAVE. We didn't force you to come here. You asked to be here. So accept the country YOU accepted.'

And now a few words about our Commander-in-Chief:

*An article from American Thinker by Geoffrey P. Hunt
Anatomy of a Failing Presidency*

Barack Obama is on track to have the most spectacularly failed presidency since Woodrow Wilson. In the modern era, we've seen several failed presidencies--led by Jimmy Carter and LBJ.. Failed presidents have one strong common trait-- they are repudiated, in the vernacular, spat out.

Of course, LBJ wisely took the exit ramp early, avoiding a shove into oncoming traffic by his own party. Richard Nixon indeed resigned in disgrace, yet his reputation as a statesman has been partially restored by his triumphant overture to China.

But, Barack Obama is failing. Failing big. Failing fast. And failing everywhere: foreign policy, domestic initiatives, and most importantly, in forging connections with the American people. The incomparable Dorothy Rabinowitz in the Wall Street Journal put her finger on it: He is failing because he has no under-

standing of the American people, and may indeed loathe them. Fred Barnes of the Weekly Standard says he is failing because he has lost control of his message, and is overexposed. Clarice Feldman of American Thinker produced a dispositive commentary showing that Obama is failing because fundamentally he is neither smart nor articulate; his intellectual dishonesty is conspicuous by its audacity and lack of shame.

But, there is something more seriously wrong: How could a new president riding in on a wave of unprecedented promise and goodwill have forfeited his tenure and become a lame duck in six months? His poll ratings are in free fall. In generic balloting, the Republicans have now seized a five point advantage. This truly is unbelievable. What's going on? No narrative. Obama doesn't have a narrative. No, not a narrative about himself. He has a self-narrative, much of it fabricated, cleverly disguised or written by someone else. But this self-narrative is isolated and doesn't connect with us. He doesn't have an American narrative that draws upon the rest of us. All successful presidents have a narrative about the American character that intersects with their own where they display a command of history and reveal an authenticity at the core of their personality that resonates in a positive endearing way with the majority of Americans. We admire those presidents whose narratives not only touch our own, but who seem stronger, wiser, and smarter than we are. Presidents we admire are aspirational peers, even those whose politics don't align exactly with our own: Teddy Roosevelt, FDR, Harry Truman, Ike, and Reagan.

But not this president. It's not so much that he's a phony, knows nothing about economics, and is historically illiterate and woefully small minded for the size of the task--all contributory of course.. It's that he's not one of us. And whatever he is, his profile is fuzzy and devoid of content, like a cardboard cutout made from delaminated corrugated paper.

Moreover, he doesn't command our respect and is unable to appeal to our own common sense. His notions of right and wrong are repugnant and how things work just don't add up. They are not existential. His descriptions of the world we live in don't make sense and don't correspond with our experience.

In the meantime, while we've been struggling to take a measurement of this man, he's dissed just

about every one of us--
financiers, energy producers,
banks, insurance executives, po-
lice officers, doctors,
nurses, hospital administrators,
post office workers, and anybody
else who has a non-green job.
Expect Obama to lament at his
last press conference in 2012:

"For those of you I offended, I
apologize. For those of you who
were not offended, you just
didn't give me enough time; if
only I'd had a second term, I
could have offended you too."

Mercifully, the Founders at the
Constitutional Convention in 1787
devised a useful remedy for such
a desperate state--staggered
terms for both houses of the leg-
islature and the executive. An
equally abominable Congress can
get voted out this year. With a
new Congress, there's always hope
of legislative gridlock until we

vote for president again two short years after that.

Yes, small presidents do fail, Barack Obama among them. The coyotes howl but the wagon train keeps rolling along.

And now, a word from our neighbor to the North:

Barack Hussein Obama: I Told You So — Yes I Did
By Howard Galganov
Montreal, Quebec , Canada
23 July 2009

When Obama won the Presidency with the help of the LEFTIST Media, Hollywood And Entertainment Liberals, Ethnic Socialists (ACORN), Stupid Non-Business Professionals and Bush Haters, I wrote: It won't take six months until the People figure this guy out and realize how horrible a mistake they've made. And when they come to that realization, the damage to the United States of America will be so great it will take a generation or more to repair - IF EVER.

The IDIOTS who not only voted for the Messiah, but also worked [hard] to promote his Lordship, are now left holding the bag.

Here are two things they will NEVER do: They will NEVER admit to making a Blunder out of all proportion by electing a snake-oil salesman with no Positive social history or management experience of any kind. They will NEVER take responsibility for the curse they've imposed upon the immediate and long-term future of their country.

In essence, the people responsible for putting this horror show in power are themselves responsible for every cataclysmic deci-

sion he makes and the Consequences thereof.

In just six months, the Messiah's polls are showing the following: On Healthcare Reform - He's going under for the third time with polling well under 50 percent, even within his own Party. Even though he might be able to muscle a Healthcare Reform Bill by using Chicago BULLY tactics against his Fellow Democrats, it will just make things worse. On Cap and Trade (Cap and Tax) - The Fat-Lady is already singing. On the Stimulus Package (Tax and Spend) - His popularity is in FREE-FALL. On the TARP package he took and ran with from President Bush -It's all but Good-Night Irene. On the closing of GITMO and "HIS" war on what he no longer wants called the War On Terrorism - He's standing in quicksand with his head just about to go under. On a compari-

son between himself and George W Bush at the same six months into their respective first term Presidencies - Bush is ahead of him in the Polls. On a comparison between He Who Walks On Water and the 12 preceding Presidents between WW II and now - Obama ranks 10th. On a Poll just Conducted, that asks who would you vote for today between Obama and Mitt Romney - It's a dead heat. Between Obama and Palin - Obama's ONLY ahead by 8 Points and she hasn't even begun to campaign. It seems to me that Obama wants to be everywhere where he shouldn't be.

He's personally invested in [totally insulting] America 's ONLY REAL Middle Eastern ally (Israel) in favor of Palestinian Despots and Murderers. He's traveling the world apologizing for the USA while lecturing others on how to do it right, when in fact and truth he has no experience at doing anything other than getting elected.

He went to the Muslim world in Egypt to declare that America IS NOT A CHRISTIAN NATION while he heaped praises on Islam, where he compared the "plight" of the Palestinians to the Holocaust.

The Russians think he's a putz, The French think he's rude.

The Germans want him to stop spending.

The Indians want him to nix his nose out of their environmental business.

The North Koreans think he's a joke, The Iranians won't acknowledge his calls.

And the British can't even come up with a comprehensive opinion of him.

As for the Chinese, he's too frightened to even glance their way. [After All, China now owns a large portion of the United States ..]

Maybe if America 's first Emperor would stay home more, travel less, and work a little bit instead of being on television just about everyday (or forget about his Wednesday Date Nights with his Amazon Wife) or stop running to "papered" Town Hall Meetings, perhaps he would have a little bit of time to do the work of the nation.

In all fairness, it wasn't HARD to be RIGHT in my prediction concerning Obama's presidency, even in its first six months, so I'm going to make yet another prediction:

OBAMA WILL PROBABLY NOT FINISH HIS 4-YEAR TERM, at least not in a conventional way.

He is such a political HORROR SHOW, and so detrimental to the USA and his Own Democratic Party, that the Democrats themselves will either FORCE him to resign or figure out a way to have him thrown out.

Who knows, maybe he really isn't a BORN US Citizen and that's a way the Democrats will be able to get rid of him. [He is a citizen, but not a naturalized citizen with both mother and father being US citizens.]

Or - MORE LIKELY THAN NOT, the Democrats will make Obama THEIR OWN LAME DUCK PRESIDENT.

I don't believe the Democrats have nearly as much love for their country as they do for their own political fortunes. And with Obama, their fortunes are rapidly becoming toast.

There is so much more that we could talk about, but the subject is the same. WE ARE GOING IN THE WRONG DIRECTION! I pray that you can see this and lend a hand in turning the country around. Both Democrats and Republicans have a duty to the American people to provide the very best service possible and one year into B.O.'s administration it is very clear that not only didn't he keep his "promises" but has allowed things to get worse. I leave you another picture that is worth thousands of words. Kind of offers an insight to our Messiah President, what he really thinks and not caring who sees it. . . .

Thank you for reading this book. I know some won't like it, but then again, the truth hurts.

Please join me in the "Tea Party" that is going on as we speak. Nothing is more important than taking back the country that our founding fathers built and restoring our standing in the world.

www.teapartynation.com
www.teapartypatriots.com

Your participation is needed.

Thanks, Ron

This Just In . . .

MY NAME IS WALT TURSKE, CLEVE-LAND OHIO

YES, I'M A BAD AMERICAN

I Am the Liberal-Progressive's Worst Nightmare

I am an American.

I am a Master Mason and believe in God.

I ride Harley Davidson Motorcycles, and believe in American products.

I believe the money I make belongs to me and my family, not some liberal governmental functionary, Democratic or Republican!

I'm in touch with my feelings and I like it that way!

I think owning a gun doesn't make you a killer; it makes you a smart American.

I think being a minority does not make you noble or victimized, and does not entitle you to anything. Get over it!

I believe that if you are selling me a Big Mac, you should do it in English.

I believe everyone has a right to pray to his or her God when and where they want to.

My heroes are John Wayne, Babe Ruth, Roy Rogers, and Willie G. Davidson,who makes the awesome Harley Davidson Motorcycles.

I don't hate the rich.. I don't pity the poor.

I know wrestling is fake and I don't waste my time watching or arguing about it.

I've never owned a slave, or was a slave. I haven't burned any witches or been persecuted by the Turks, and neither have you! So, shut up already.

I believe if you don't like the way things are here, go back to where you came from and change your own country!

This is AMERICA ..We like it the way it is!

If you were born here and don't like it you are free to move to any Socialist country that will have you.

I want to know which church is it, exactly,

where the Reverend Jesse Jackson preaches, where he gets his money, and why he is always part of the problem and not the solution.

Can I get an AMEN on that one?

I also think the cops have the right to pull you over if you're breaking the law, regardless of what color you are.

And, no, I don't mind having my face shown on my driver's license.

I think it's good.... And I'm proud that 'God' is written on my money.

I think if you are too stupid to know how a ballot works, I don't want you deciding who should be running the most powerful nation in the world for the next four years.

I dislike those people standing in the intersections trying to sell me stuff or trying to guilt me into making 'donations' to their cause.......Get a Job and do your part!

I believe that it doesn't take a village to raise a child, it takes two parents..

I believe 'illegal' is illegal no matter what the lawyers think.

I believe the American flag should be the only one allowed in AMERICA !

If this makes me a BAD American, then yes, I'm a BAD American.

We want our country back!

WE   NEED   GOD   BACK
IN   OUR   COUNTRY!!

WE LIVE IN THE LAND OF THE FREE,
ONLY BECAUSE OF THE BRAVE!

May God Bless You All

www.ingramcontent.com/pod-product-compliance
Lightning Source LLC
Chambersburg PA
CBHW050539280326
41933CB00011B/1643